I Say Yes

Reclaiming Respect and Love for Life

Cathy Courtney

Copyright © 2018 Cathy Courtney.

www.cathycourtney.org

All rights reserved. No part of this book may be used or reproduced by any means, graphic, electronic, or mechanical, including photocopying, recording, taping or by any information storage retrieval system without the written permission of the author except in the case of brief quotations embodied in critical articles and reviews.

This book is a work of non-fiction. Unless otherwise noted, the author and the publisher make no explicit guarantees as to the accuracy of the information contained in this book and in some cases, names of people and places have been altered to protect their privacy.

Balboa Press books may be ordered through booksellers or by contacting:

Balboa Press
A Division of Hay House
1663 Liberty Drive
Bloomington, IN 47403
www.balboapress.com
1 (877) 407-4847

Because of the dynamic nature of the Internet, any web addresses or links contained in this book may have changed since publication and may no longer be valid. The views expressed in this work are solely those of the author and do not necessarily reflect the views of the publisher, and the publisher hereby disclaims any responsibility for them.

The author of this book does not dispense medical advice or prescribe the use of any technique as a form of treatment for physical, emotional, or medical problems without the advice of a physician, either directly or indirectly. The intent of the author is only to offer information of a general nature to help you in your quest for emotional and spiritual well-being. In the event you use any of the information in this book for yourself, which is your constitutional right, the author and the publisher assume no responsibility for your actions.

Any people depicted in stock imagery provided by Getty Images are models, and such images are being used for illustrative purposes only. Certain stock imagery © Getty Images.

Print information available on the last page.

ISBN: 978-1-9822-1090-8 (sc)
ISBN: 978-1-9822-1089-2 (hc)
ISBN: 978-1-9822-1088-5 (e)

Library of Congress Control Number: 2018910148

Balboa Press rev. date: 09/10/2018

Contents

Dedication ix
Foreword xiii
Introduction xvii

No Denying 1
Walking the Talk 4
Guilt 5
Current 6
Pullback 7
Missing Him 8
Anniversary 9
Do I Care 10
Pain 11
I Don't Know You 12
Decision 13
Opinions 14
Low Road 15
Dues 16
Lost 17
Storm 18
Spinning 20

Drowning	22
Warning	24
Waiting room	25
Same Old	26
A Dangerous Choice	27
The Players	28
Fortitude	29
Responsibility	30
Ledger	32
Protection	33
The Ego	35
Dream	36
No Us	38
Impatience	40
An Ache	41
Lifeline	42
Plea	44
Tough Love	46
Labor Pains	48
The Edge	49
Pillar	50
R.i.P.	51
Yum	52
Breaking the Bindings	53
Your Work	55
Lift Off	57

Payment	58
Moments in Time	59
Jumping	61
Action	62
Discovering	63
Learning	64
Teamwork	65
Reconnecting	66
Common Denominator	67
Being Human	68
Falling in Love	69
Acknowledgements	71
Further Reading	73
Index Of Poems	75
Endnotes	79

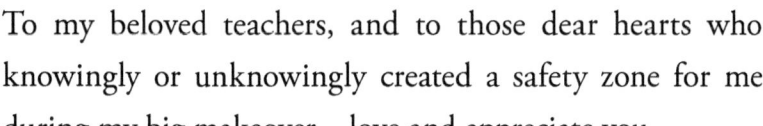

Dedication

To my beloved teachers, and to those dear hearts who knowingly or unknowingly created a safety zone for me during my big makeover – love and appreciate you.

Anahata (Sanskrit)—unstruck, continuous inner resonance, the heart, the heart center, the inner divine melody.[1]

Foreword

Adversity is an indisputable fact of life. A common reaction to adversity is to bear it as best we can—some do it better than others—and move on with life.

There are, however, those rare individuals who not only gain wisdom from life's challenges but also choose to inspire, enlighten, and enrich others with their insights. Enter Cathy Courtney and the end of her marriage.

Ask those who have been through a divorce, and they will tell you it rocks the foundation of your being and leaves you feeling lonely, flawed, undesirable, enraged, and hopeless, to name just a few emotions. In her book *I Say Yes,* Cathy eloquently describes her own personal transformation from fear to an empowered woman of courage. By sharing her darkness and recovery, she provides an intelligent blueprint for you to do the same.

Cathy was determined to confront everything she was up against—the loss of power and strength, and the inability to ward off thoughts of defeat. How did she do this? By looking beneath the surface with laserlike honesty, the guidance of a few trusted people, and her spirituality. Without illusions, she explored her past and developed the courage to change her behavior. Cathy learned that she was blocked in certain areas of her life, and in order to move beyond the ghosts of her past, she needed to confront her fears, insecurities, and regrets.

In other words, she took ownership of the self she'd relinquished in her marriage.

In *I Say Yes,* Cathy shows us how she took responsibility for moving beyond victimization. The good news, she tells us, is that by developing the courage to stop blaming others and becoming personally accountable, the magic of healing takes place.

If you are facing the adversity of divorce, you must read Cathy's beautiful poems and heed her sagacious advice: Take control of your life and liberate yourself from the past.

Deborah P. Hecker, PhD
Washington, DC

The truth, as I see it, is that everything you think, say, and do is a choice.

—Wayne Dyer[2]

The poems in this book are the result of a reluctantly chosen journey through the ending of my decades' long marriage.

If you are at a turning point, struggling, and perhaps doubting your ability to get to the other side, or even going through a dark night of the soul, I am here to encourage you and say: Yes you can. You can do it. You can get through. I did, so I know you can as well. The poems supported and guided me through what was a repeatedly challenging time – maybe, just maybe, a word or a phrase will resonate and support you.

Introduction

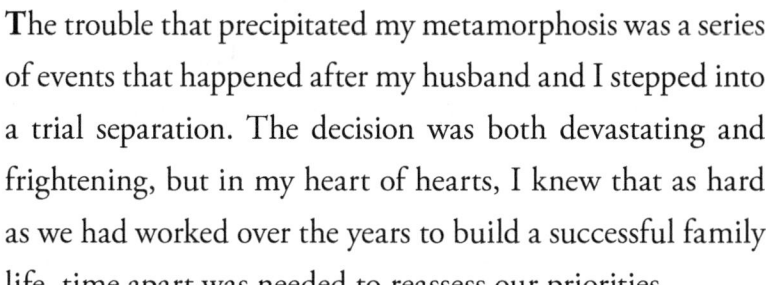

The trouble that precipitated my metamorphosis was a series of events that happened after my husband and I stepped into a trial separation. The decision was both devastating and frightening, but in my heart of hearts, I knew that as hard as we had worked over the years to build a successful family life, time apart was needed to reassess our priorities.

While I had never been close to a marriage breakdown before, I was determined to handle things in a manner that was as positive as possible. Apart from any other considerations, with children establishing their own lives, it was important to continue as we had done previously and lead by example. I had the tools, I thought, for this to become the reality.

With a deep-seated belief in the innate connectedness of everything in the world, living from a heart-centered place of respect, kindness, and integrity was foundational for me. The belief was underpinned by my conviction in the ultimate benevolence of the universe and the unfailing support of Grace. On a very practical front, my lifelong work with nonprofits and volunteers had solidified my understanding of the strength inherent in cohesive teamwork, and by extension, the importance of resolving conflicts in a way that achieved the best outcome for everyone involved.

The months rolled by and it became obvious that I had made a mistake: I had not taken into account the possible negative effects of separating on a trial basis. I found myself living uneasily, in a constant state of flux with no substantive conversations about resolving the future. The insidious stress began to take its toll. A type of mental fogginess descended, undermining my ability to think clearly. Physically, the price being extracted was becoming impossible to hide - I could not keep food down and had lost weight, and lack of sleep resulted in constant tiredness. If this was not enough, panic attacks began.

As the eighteen month mark came and went, my self-confidence and my hold on the goals and convictions I held so dear were faltering. Appalled and humiliated at my inability to cope, I disconnected from my network of family and community and retreated into myself. With the exception of weekly counseling sessions, I had all but withdrawn from life as I once knew it. Still the downward spiral continued. I cancelled my counseling appointments, then crumpled in on myself and became a me unimaginable, a near-frozen, emotional mess. It was not a healthy place to be.

Yet the spirit is strong, the sense of survival powerful. In a profound ah-ha moment, I saw, really saw, what I was doing to myself and remembered all the supports and tools I had been given and learned over the years – my faith, my yoga, the different contemplation and self-inquiry techniques I had not only learned, but taught. I had experience in conflict resolution meetings for goodness sake. It was time to do what was necessary, so I took myself by the shoulders, and gave myself a good talking to – it was enough already.

At heart, I am a practical person. In spite of what some have called my woo-woo tendencies toward spiritual exploration, I am sensible and down to earth. I had not always been in the boardroom or yoga hall. I had managed five international moves (four of them with young children), I had flipped nine of fourteen homes (I could use a hand drill, hammer a nail, and paint a ceiling with the confidence of a professional.) Yes, it was past time to pick myself up, adjust my attitude, and start taking some action that would help move me out of the quagmire into which I had descended.

The decision to leave the emotional shambles behind did not mean that my way ahead would be easy; it would be another nine months before I felt strong enough to finally approach a lawyer. However, it did mean that movement was happening, and given my numbed state at this point, any shift was a shift in the right direction.

I was soon drawing on every piece of knowledge I had absorbed, scraping the barrel at times, trying to find the presence of mind, the detached and focused attention, needed to tackle the untangling of our personal affairs.

As new determination took root, the mind fog started to clear, and glimpses of the past began to appear. Abandoning the streams of *poor me* that I had been flirting with for too long, I looked at my part in the relationship and saw damaging undercurrents in the shape of well-camouflaged and deep-seated insecurities. Unwittingly, I had established two seriously flawed coping mechanisms in the relationship.

The first was a habit of escaping into busy-ness. I was a master at it. If my diary was overflowing with commitments, I was a happy camper; if not, I made sure that the gaps were filled. The busier I was, the better. I had created the perfect justification for pushing back on dealing directly with personal issues that challenged my comfort level.

The second was another escape route - an excessive optimism, a pervasive Pollyanna attitude that enabled me to always see the bright side and avoid having to address almost anything that was uncomfortable in the marriage.

Looking deeper to discover what was beneath these habits was sobering. I was confident and at ease when leading high level meetings or speaking at large events, yet in my closest relationship, the marriage, I had serious confidence and self-worth issues. And there was something else. Admitting to these, and the underlying questions surrounding self-respect was not easy. "Surely, not!" I argued with myself. "Surely, yes," my wise-self responded. Clearly, it was time for more work.

As is often the way when a decision to change is made, support, at times unexpected, shows up.

Family and friends from whom I had removed myself were in contact and there for me. People I hardly knew let me know they were around if I needed a ready ear or cup of coffee. In no time at all, I felt surrounded by love and objective support which in a sense, scooped me up and deposited me in a type of unspoken safety zone. Buoyed by this nurturing, the scales began to rebalance: more of the heaviness dropped away and a greater willingness and confidence arose. I reached another threshold: it was time to become my own best friend and my most courageous cheer squad.

Life pinged into action.

A voracious appetite for exploration surfaced. If something pulled me toward it, I listened to my gut instinct and said yes without stopping to scrutinize its benefits, as I would have done previously. Surprise, surprise, one thing led to another. Books steered me into different ways of thinking. My inbox took me to online and in-person courses. Webinars exposed me to new teachers, workshops and developing technologies. There were many roads with multiple opportunities, all leading me forward.

My daily habits (the good ones) needed to be reinvigorated. The quality of my diet and eating habits improved; and to help curb my night wandering, I started a regimen of non-habit-forming sleep aids.

As my energy rebuilt, I prioritized exercise. Hatha yoga was a constant – the careful pacing of the movements combined with the rhythm of the breath gave me an hour of moving meditation. This was important, because the sitting meditation I so loved had become an unexpected and frustrating challenge - both body and mind were rebelling at the idea of sitting quietly for the usual forty or so minutes.

Tai chi lessons took me for a time into the world of martial arts, with the tai chi master teaching me to use the breath differently from yoga – harnessing it to release powerful physical movements through my arms and legs strong enough to split apart wooden boards. I loved that.

I started riding a pushbike (a cute one) as well. Originally bought somewhat begrudgingly to help me get around (I was without a car at this time), I learned to love riding it. It's no joke, though, when I say that the hardest thing about transitioning to pedal-power, was accepting the fact that my wardrobe had to change. In my new push-biker world, I needed to trade in my classic beige look for bike pants and my first ever baseball cap.

A new friend encouraged me towards a creative outlet and loaned me an easel and some paints. That led me to a camera, where the one-pointed focus of peering down the lens was another great way of taking me out of the whirligig of the mind and into a quiet, expanded place.

Recognizing how quickly my mind would drift into a whorl of negativities, or what I called *the land of imagined scenarios*, I employed all types of more immediate interruptions as reminders to reboot and drop into the present moment - forward bends, cold showers, and even very loud singing worked to trick the mind. Handel's "Alleluia Chorus" or the Queen classic "We Are the Champions" are fantastically therapeutic at full throttle.

Within these strategies there were also light bulb moments. In a particularly luminous one, I realized that the negativities themselves were not the issue, rather it was being stuck in them that was the problem; and more, that what I had always regarded as the less than perfect or bad parts of me, were in fact integral to who I was, and that I could make them my friends by using them as doorways to explore another layer (or two) of what made me tick. What a concept!

Throughout all of this inner digging, books were a bastion. I devoured untold numbers of them, drawing on the knowledge and wisdom of so many incredibly talented minds.

Inspiring quotations began to litter my walls as reminders to stay centered and present.

One in particular became my touchstone: "There is no power greater than doing the right thing in the present moment." It was said to have been translated from an ancient yogic text called the *Yoga-Vasishtha*: The words struck me as being brilliantly succinct and sensible. They told me what to do and when to do it without any wiggle room at all. I made doing the right thing in the present moment my intention, attitude, and the approach I would take in all my actions and interactions. I fell off the perch a few times, but the support these words gave me was second only to the other quote.

This one came in the form of a memory. Out of the blue one day, words I had heard in church (which I had attended only occasionally for years) started reverberating through me: "The greatest of these is love ... The greatest of these is love."[3] Soon, eight-inch letters spelling the word *Love* were posted around the house, reminding me again and again that when everything is said and done (including forgiveness), love above all else is what matters. Living it thoughout this time might have been a challenge, but it was also an imperative.

One daily outlet was indispensable: journal writing. I filled tiny books, large books, spiral pads, legal pads, jazzy journals, and plain journals. Lined or unlined, it didn't matter. Only the writing was important. Journaling was where my hidden truths emerged and where I allowed myself to explore the hard questions, especially when I found my principles at odds with my thoughts or my actions.

It also gave expression to the hidden parts of me that I

denied or was ashamed about. While I was gaining a huge amount from my reinstated counseling sessions, the deep stuff was still hard to vocalize. In writing down unfiltered inner comment, it became easier to talk about.

Among the outpouring poems started pushing hard to be released. Not planned, nor carefully crafted, the poems were entities in themselves. Their advent surprised me. Poetry had never been a medium of creativity for me. Yet there they were, unheralded, in a very real way insisting themselves into being. Without question, my soul had found a way to teach me, and I had found a way to listen.

The poetry became my rock and the deep heart of my long, winding road to transformation.

Seven years after beginning, all the legalities were finally done. By this time, everyone, even my lawyers, heaved a sigh of relief.

The experience was hard, but perhaps hardest on the children. They had no choice but to walk the tightrope of trying not to take sides, adjusting to new concepts about their parents, all the while having to deal with their own grieving for the loss of our once tight family unit. Unsurprisingly, the recalibration has had its moments, but the new definition of what it means to be our family is settling in.

The journey has changed me, radically I think - lighter in spirit, with a new strength, willingness and enthusiasm.

Walls of defensiveness have dropped away, resulting in a

softening of my vulnerability and a corresponding growth in my openness. This in turn has increased how I value and appreciate the time and effort of others, and, too, my own. Fundamental things, such as facing up to issues or problems in a timely manner; understanding that speaking up appropriately and expressing my genuine opinion is not only a courtesy to others, but a courtesy to myself as well; accepting kindnesses in a simple, uncomplicated way, makes it easier for others to offer and for me to ask if help is needed; I am not going through my days apologizing to people unnecessarily; and the self-critical *shoulds* are dropping away.

The lessons in the power of the present moment have been profound. Where once, being in the now for me centered around different yoga and Meditation or prayer practices, this journey gave me the opportunity to experience what happens to one's inner capacity when being in the present becomes an habitual part of day-to-day life.

The work of forgiveness continues and has its own demands, placing me on a collision course with all those judgmental bits and pieces that seem only too happy to hang on inside. Something comes up; I do the work, breathe a sigh of relief, and move on. Months will go by, and then out of the blue, boom—something will trigger a memory, the little gremlins will pop their heads up, and there's still more to be done. It is a little like scraping off barnacles really.

The convictions I held so dear at the beginning of the

process about the innate and essential nature of connectedness and heart-centered living are even deeper now. Although I can't imagine, even in my wildest dreams, consciously choosing this particular journey for my big makeover, the irony is that there is no way I would go back and exchange the me I am now for the me I was before.

It feels good to be able to acknowledge the distance traveled, the effort made, and the lessons learned. How incongruous It is, that in spite of the painful nature of events at the time, I am now filled with awe and gratitude for the entire process and its outcome. A tempest of apparently perfect proportions was created for my growth.

Such is the revolutionary nature of life: things happen, and we get to deal with them in the best way we can.

And so I say again: if you are struggling, doubting your ability to get to the other side, or going through your own dark night of the soul, I am here to encourage you and to say:

You can do it.

Yes.

You. Can. Do. It. ⌘

No Denying

Change was stirring
Uneasy
Fearful
I applied the long honed expertise
Moved and shrugged the inklings back
Down
To their shadowy resting place
Uncomfortable but familiar
Not this time sister
Not this time
Out of left field
The tempest hit with the fury of a force five hurricane
It blew
Blew until all my carefully constructed shelters were obliterated
The stifling familiarity
Erased
This time there was there was nowhere to hide
This time there was no denying
The force picked me up

Instead of turning me back as before
It pitched me forward
Terrified
I tried to push towards the pieces that were my life
An invisible wall blocked the way
And I knew
I knew
I was being held exactly
Where I was supposed to be
As the understanding seeped in
The pain began
A physical rending of absolutely essential separation
I wailed for what was lost
Then
Silence
I was spent
Nothingness held me in its womb
Whispering
A voice leaned in
You can do it you know
You can do it
Open your eyes
Look
You are so close
It was clear
My future had become weary with impatience

No longer taking No for an answer
Had placed itself
Squarely in my face
Soft now
Adjusting to the light
Choices
Hungry for attention
Lay before me in a dazzling array of shapes and colors
Without doubt
It was time
It was time for me
To say yes
Agonizing with sheer necessity
I let go and cried
I say yes
I say yes ⌘

Walking the Talk

This situation challenges me
It puts me in my own line of fire
To live up to every single belief about inherent goodness
Others'
My own
It dangles itself
Smirking
Fine for the good times but what about the bad
Let's see how you go with this shall we
How much of what you have talked about
How much of what you've taught
How much of it really is true for you
Can you walk your talk
Will you have the stamina
I think so
No
I will
I mean yes
I will ⌘

Guilt

Why is it
That every single time I try to express myself in terms of My
Wants or needs
I am wracked by feelings of guilt
What is this
Why do I feel I am to blame
Responsible
Why am I
Afraid of looking
Admitting
His part in this
What is hidden in this darkness
Where is the courage
Take off the blinders
Open your eyes
And look
Dear one
Look ⌘

Current

Intent on its work
Of pulling us apart
The current drags
Longing for the old sweetness
I resist
Amongst frustration and disappointment
But even here
A glimmer
Recognition of the falsehood
Making way for a rising anticipation
Excited to meet the person
We
Never
Noticed
Me to be ⌘

Pullback

I can feel
You
Pulling back
Further
Away
Going
Soon gone
Parts resist
Clutching
Longing for the old
Sweetness
The love
That was never wholly there ⌘

Missing Him

I miss my friend

More than I could have conceived

But then how could I have known

Or for that matter

Not known

Only experience gives true understanding

Then I wonder

Deep down

If what I really miss

Is not him at all

But the idea of him ⌘

Anniversary

What to say
With me here
You there
By choice and agreement
Married
Still Married
What am I thinking
Or am I thinking at all
With all my heart
I try not to be resentful
For the fruit of that
Is my own destruction
When
When
Will you do what clearly must be done
Soon
Just not today ⌘

Do I Care

Contrary to appearances
I am not a mumbling mess
I am getting through this
And I am doing it well
It is just that sometimes I have a meltdown
Yesterday was hard
Realizing he's a lot further down the track than he admits
Makes me want to throw up
Do I care
Yes
I care a lot
But I have to admit
Part of me doesn't at all
Soon
I hope
None of me will ⌘

Pain

Even knowing the truth
The necessity
I am completely unprepared for the relentless pain
This tearing apart from my mate
I turn myself inside out
Trying to make sense of it
To understand
What would have made a difference
What I did wrong
But as the reality unfolds
I shatter amidst the roar of divulgence
My mind
My heart
Pulverized
Numbness is a blessed relief
I check out
Go through the motions like an automaton
Not knowing
Not caring
When or where it will all end ⌘

I Don't Know You

Who are you
This changing tone
Grudging
Hard done by
Poor me attitude
A you
Unfamiliar
New phrasings
Expressions of a stranger
Not the person I knew
It is close
Nearly time to call it quits
To release each other
In the end
You will have what you wanted
Or will you ⌘

Decision

Reluctance
Protestations
Variations cried on the same old theme
Have fallen away
I have made the decision
Cast the die
And now
Wrapped in the stillness of preparation
Emotions at half staff
Right action is all that remains
Balance
Simpatico with the rhythm of the breath
Is the fight
That must be fought

Opinions

Concerned for me
Concerned for you
Well-meaning friends
Judge
Advise
Destabilize
Well-meaning friends
Concerned for me
Concerned for you
Are seriously exhausting ⌘

Low Road

Knowing that blame is futile
There are times
Like now
When the low road calls
Loudly
And
I want
Very
Very badly
To shout from the rooftops
What you
What all of you
Are doing is
Completely
Utterly
Wrong ⌘

Dues

In the end
Each and every one
Will shoulder their own burden of responsibility
Who am I to put a percentage on it
All I really know is
That the brunt will be borne
Somehow
Somewhere
Sometime
Dues will be exacted ⌘

Lost

Who am I
Who am I
Am I now defined by who I am not
The rug has been pulled with such determination
Life has exploded
Family, friends, community
Even country
Scattered
To end up who knows where
Through inattention, manipulation or fate
Or any combination thereof
Taken
Put out to pasture
One breath of shocked understanding
Equals
Plans, dreams snuffed out
Who am I now
Now that I am not
Who I thought I was ⌘

Storm

Sometimes there is a quantum leap

From positive to negative

From calm to fury

Before I know it

The whirling tempest hits

Sticks

Like treacle

Self-control vanishes

And another steps from the shadows into my form

Thinking and saying things that come from who knows where

Things that I want to think are not me

Have nothing to do with me

Yet in my heart of hearts

I know

Long repressed

They do

Then almost as quickly

I'm back
To the me I am trying to be
Breathing
Breathing ⌘

Spinning

The question haunts me still
Who am I
At an esoteric level
I get that I am all or part
Of the boundaryless whole
The eternal
One
It should be enough
Yet
With the me that I was
All but liquidated
I feel
Absent
Roles, responsibilities, functions
Removed
Who is this me that is left
I have no idea
Perhaps it doesn't matter

Maybe the question itself is irrelevant
And knowing
That I am
Is enough
Enough for now
To survive on
Perhaps
I'll tell you tomorrow
Perhaps ⌘

Drowning

Tired

Worn weary

Right to the edges of my soul

Trying to make my way

Is it the years of effort

The trying so hard to spin straw into gold

Or the long pretense that the

For better

Was really the

For worse

Oh you dear brave face

All the time showing the world that you were a goodwife

When in truth

You just never mustered the courage

To stand up and say

Enough

And now

In this stage of almost freedom
Held by chains of neither here nor there
I am
Drowning
In a new sea ⌘

Warning

A confusing

Sad

Sad

State of being

Oddly comforting

Warning

Beware

Agonizing is dangerously seductive

Agonizing

Is

Dangerously

Seductive ⌘

Waiting room

Somewhere
It is somewhere
The way
Out of the darkness into which I have plunged
Frustrated beyond words
I know
I will
Wait
A little longer ⌘

Same Old

A journal
Written long ago
Memories of despair
Forever old
Flooded in
How those words had struggled to find their way
I muse at the futility of all that effort
It leaves me wondering
Why
Why did it take me so long
To see
The truth
The reality
Known as
Used by date ⌘

A Dangerous Choice

Driving towards what was to be our home
Pondering possessions carefully culled
Familiarity and instinct
Keeping the highway in focus
Not good
Pay attention
Take a breath
And another
Refocus
The leaden mind
Tries escape
Reverberating dissonance again
And fails
Stop the car
Get out from behind this wheel
Now ⌘

The Players

All this vitriol
Is distracting
Turning you in the wrong direction
It is easy to find fault with the other
Be very aware
That there were two people in this relationship
And whether or not it is palatable to you
Two people
Played their parts here ⌘

Fortitude

A glimpse
An almost-whisper
The world stills
My whole being
Pauses
Straining to hear
I release the need into the silence
The syllables find their way
The message
Clears
Then sinks into my cells
Fortitude
Remember
Fortitude ⌘

Responsibility

Who
Now
In this present moment
Is really responsible
As the shards slowly re-form
Into facets of understanding
I see my own contaminants
The seditious effect of extreme optimism
The staggering ability to live in denial
Counter to everything I believe
I had gifted myself
To the demon powerlessness
Well
No longer
Drawing the line
My mind slows
The notion of the outer falls away
And with crystal clarity

I recognize
That this battle
Is
Within ⌘

Ledger

I wonder
Do our decades together
Founder on the measure of the dollar
Does all that we have been
Find its final grappling
Scorched on the value of goods and chattels
In columns of debtors and creditors
Or could it be
That the untangling
Has the currency to show the way forward
Pushing so many buttons
That in order to hear
Over the screeching clamor of the collection agency
There is no alternative
Pay Attention
And Listen
Very
Very
Carefully ⌘

Protection

Mostly I'm ok
Get the green check mark
But every now and then the stealth bomber strikes again
Equilibrium vaporizes
And I plummet
Into the pit
Of furious mind-numbing bitterness
The rage
Tantalizing
The agony
Tempting to indulge
But the warrior
Bent on the better way
Rises
And wields high
Her blade of protection
She cries a fearsome

Get ye gone
And I'm rescued again
Worn weary
But thankful to have another byway cleared ⌘

The Ego

I am learning
That it is not always about me
Who knew I had become so introspective
Me Me Me
In scrutinizing responsibility
Apportioning blame
The ego is a curly compadre
Focused on its own view of protectiveness
Remember
It does not always align
To attain
Right
Outcome
Your watchfulness is vital ⌘

Dream

Stirred by some unseen movement
I nuzzle my face into your body
Breathe in the sleeping you
In the distant dimness
I sigh
Content in the protection of your arms
The hairs on your chest
Matted by the pressure of me
Tickle my face and cause me to shift
Snuggling closer still
I sense your absence
Then smile in anticipation of your returning warmth
But your whispered
Home, home
Doesn't come
My sleep-dulled brain
Starts to connect the dots
It is the dream
Sweet reverie turns to a flood of overwhelming sadness
I remember where you are

Desperate with self-preservation
I beg
Help
Help me
Please ⌘

No Us

Uneasy awareness

Disquiet

Is it hurt

Or something else

Reluctantly

I admit

It's the something else

The dark-shadowed face of resentment

The little sister of bitterness

The engine room of torment

Poor you

Indulgence beckons

Poor you

Then the rise

No way

Not for me the destructive vortex of the down-turned mouth

The exit

Complete Acceptance

Is there

Close

I finally declare
There
Is
No
Us ⌘

Impatience

At some level I know
I have the power to transcend this
I will emerge from the maelstrom
Whole and new
I just wish it would happen
Soon
No
Not soon
I wish it would happen
Right
Now ⌘

An Ache

Today my heart aches for this person
This bygone husband, lover and sometime friend
Who surely
Deep down
Must want
To do the right thing
Yet seems to shudder with the pull of divergent directions
I pray that he will be able to find his way
Wade through the plethora of demands
To his own peaceful place ⌘

Lifeline

Oh groan
Not again
The poor me words surge unrelenting
Why now
With the light so close
Is it habit
A reluctance to let the lure of hurt go
Or is it more
Brooding on the old alley song
Thoughts spiral down
Spilling all my good intentions
Into hellish darkness
The black cell echoing the chant gleefully
No way out
No way out
Sucked into again casual disregard for my life
Hopelessness cuts deep
Then rescue arrives
Exasperation
The heat turns up

To a furious broiling
And I understand
I get it
The self-serving evil ones
Will never give up
Will always be there
Looking for a gap
To slink in and sabotage
The good work
Remembering
Calm washes over
I turn within
Reaching for the radiance
Of the lifeline ⌘

Plea

Please God

Let this be done soon

So my life can be filled with people who are real

Who

Respect

And

Live

With Kindness

Who

Love

With Integrity

But the plea doubles back

If this is your prayer

Live its truth

You

Must live

With Respect

And kindness
And integrity
You
Must live
In
Love ⌘

Tough Love

Where have you gone
Yes, you
Not him
Have you dumped yourself in the leavings
Are you toying with what's deceased
Delaying processing
Feeding the putrefaction
Get up
Now
Start moving
Take a step
And another
That is all
That is required for living
Understand this
Extermination is the work
Requisite

Essential
For living
Allow it
The chains will release ⌘

Labor Pains

The lurching feeling
Pounces again when I least expect it
The destructive destabilization
That has to go
It has to go
It's time now
The use-by date has been reached
The gut wrenching waves no longer serve
Labor pains
Full term
Birth Day
Welcome to your world, dear one
Yay and Yes
A thousand times
Yay and Yes ⌘

The Edge

The days are easier
The passage of time perhaps
Or simply an exhaustion
Born of effort
That forces the letting go
Knowing the only way forward
Is held in
One
Single
Step
Off the edge
Into the abyss
The terrifying place
Acceptance
Of a future
Unknown ⌘

Pillar

Be wise

Get understanding

The first teacher wrote

At last

Unveiled understanding

All I need to be

Is here

Present

Resting in the heart

Trusting

Whether I remember or not

The Pillar

Is

Always

Available

For

Leaning ⌘

R.i.P.

I have cried
Wept
Grieving
For the death of the me I was before
Lost from the start
This dear one
Struggled so hard
To be all she should
All she could
On her grave
I leave
Flowers of gratitude
For her love
Her devotion
Rest in peace
Precious one
Rest in peace ⌘

Yum

Woke early today
Wrapped in a sense of contentment
The familiar sadness absent
Replaced
With a new world
Of not-thought
For the first time in what seems like forever
I luxuriated in drowsiness ⌘

Breaking the Bindings

Who is this new me emerging
Scattered
At sixes and sevens
Blazing new trails
Snail-like at times
Then fast-forward at breakneck speed
The energy appears
Then is spent
Curious
I would have thought
This unfolding would be more measured
But not to be it seems
It is sort of fun
Witnessing all this
Push-me pull-you growth
It feels good
To be

Unbound
Unhampered
Learning to be free
Learning to be me ⌘

Your Work

A waking sigh
More sleep
Please
The distant voice wins attention
Barely there
I hear
You are here to become alive
You are here to become alive
Awake now
Alert
Listening to a gathering crescendo
You are here to become alive
Hear me
You are here to become alive
Is this what all this is about
Everything
The good
The bad
And the downright ugly
Is for this purpose

For me
To become alive
To wake up
And become alive
Far out ⌘

Lift Off

Reaching in
Not knowing but alert
The undercurrent of something big
There
The flash
Move
Run
Pick up the pace
Double the effort
Determined
I round towards the arc
Throwing myself at its edges
Holding on for dear life
Slowly
Gently
I am lifted
Warmth
Wraps me in Love
And I
Exhale ⌘

//
Payment

At last
Owings nearly paid
Books balanced
In the eye of my knowing
Price
In perfect measure
Extracted
In
Now
Weightless form ⌘

Moments in Time

Countless times every day

A fragment of time

Presents itself

Beckons saying

Come

Enter the moment

Merge into the present

Experience your power

I am either alert to it or it is gone

The moments are so frequent

Common

That most slip by unrecognized

But every now and then

One catches in a pause of awareness

Projecting me into

Three sixty degrees

Of unthought accord

Present

Moment

Space

Where all that exists is in balance
Where the potential of fathomless capacity
Is open for business
Awaiting my collaboration
In this very moment ⌘

Jumping

When in doubt
The second teacher said
Jump
Honor the lesson I think
Gulping
Weighing discrimination
Breathing in
I allow it
And jump
Into the free fall
A silky closing over
Merging into rightness
The linear measure of time blurs
Right action becomes its own propulsion
In this place
Anything
Everything
Is
Possible ⌘

Action

It is near
The completion
Days perhaps
Or Weeks
Who knows
This anticipation
Is a good feeling
It's impossible to know what's around the corner
But life is presenting itself again
And it feels so very good
To be on the move once more ⌘

Discovering

Rousing
Reaching out
Tentatively testing
Allowing and playful
Finding delight
In unfettered exchange
What has gone before is the very antithesis of this
And highlights the polarity
Shadow
Light
This sweet refrain
Is filled with life
It requires no measure
It simply is ⌘

Learning

Intersections

Everywhere

All leading forward into freedom

Freedom to be me

The person

Who was always

Willing

But had to learn

That

To hold on

Often

We

Must

First

Let go ⌘

Teamwork

This morning
I noticed
The breath as it moved
In
Out
In
Out
The heart pumped
Baboom
Baboom
Baboom
I was awed by the
Inner effortlessness
Of body parts engaged in the collective energy
Of
Perfect
Natural
Teamwork ⌘

Reconnecting

Melding
We are melding
After the interminable winter
The body
Yawns and stretches
Savoring in its newfound self
Surprised to be
Witnessing
Welcoming
Affection ⌘

Common Denominator

Oneness
In essence
No me
No you
No us
No them
The common denominator
Diversity within unity
Unity within diversity
All in one
Source ⌘

Being Human

A good place to be
Or perhaps simply
A place to be
Is
Present
Beyond
Where people and events rest without judgment
Where right and wrong are non-existent
Where purity is an anomaly
Transcended
And
Being
Is
Truly
Human ⌘

Falling in Love

Half alive
Volume turned down
Keeping up appearances
Making way as I thought I should
Doing the best I knew
Not wrong
Just the way it was
Not now
This new me discovery
Is captivating
I think I am
Falling
A little in love
With myself
Yes, myself
The me of my heart
I am
Buoyed with
Respect for
The effort

And
The exquisite shades
Of the me
That I am
The me
I am
Growing to be ⌘

Acknowledgements

Dr. Deborah Hecker, deep thanks for writing the foreword to *I Say Yes*. I am touched and honored. My readers, I am beyond grateful for your generous and frank input. I appreciate you all!

Further Reading

Chidvilasananda, Gurumayi. *Sadhana of the Heart: A Collection of Talks on Spiritual Life.* Chennai: Citsakti Publications, 2007.

Comte-Sponville, Andre. *A Short Treatise on the Great Virtues: The Uses of Philosophy in Everyday Life.* Catherine Temerson, trans. London: Vintage, 2003.

Dyer, Wayne. *Excuses Begone! How to Change Life Long Defeating Patterns.* New York: Hay House, Inc., 2011.

Edwards, Michaelle. *YogAlign – Pain Free Yoga from Your Inner Core.* Hanalei: Hihimanu Press, 2011.

Hecker, Deborah Potashnik. *Torn Between Two Loves: How Entrepreneurs Can Successfully Commit to Both Business and Significant Others.* Boca Raton: Yours, Mine, Ours, Publishing Company, 2016.

Hecker, Deborah Potashnik. *Who Am I Without My Partner? Post-Divorce Healing and Rediscovering Your SELF*. Denver: Graham publishing Group, 2013.

Lipton, Bruce. *The Biology of Belief.* New York: Hay House, Inc., 2008

Myss, Carolyn. *Defy Gravity: Healing Beyond the Bounds of Reason*. New York: Hay House, Inc., 2009.

Rydall, Derek. *Emergence – Seven Steps for Radical Life Change*. New York: Atria Paperpack, 2015.

Index Of Poems

A Dangerous Choice

An Ache

Action

Anniversary

Being human

Breaking the Bindings

Common Denominator

Current

Decision

Discovering

Do I Care

Dream

Drowning

Dues

Falling in Love

Fortitude

Guilt

I Don't Know You

Impatience

Jumping

Labor Pains

Learning

Ledger

Lifeline

Lift Off

Lost

Low Road

Missing Him

Moments in Time

No Denying

No Us

Opinions

Pain

Payment

Pillar

Plea

Protection

Pullback

Reconnecting

Responsibility

R.I.P.

Same Old

Spinning

Storm

Teamwork

The Edge

The Ego
The Players
Tough Love
Waiting Room
Warning
Walking the Talk
Your Work
Yum

Endnotes

[1] John Grimes, *A Concise Dictionary of Indian Philosophy: Sanskrit Terms Defined in English* (New York: State University of New York, 1996).

[2] Wayne Dyer, *Excuses Begone! How to Change Life Long Defeating Patterns* (New York: Hay House, Inc., 2011).

[3] 1 Corinthians 13:13 International Standard Version, Release 2.1 (The ISV Foundation, 1996).